Pebble® Plus

T0050896

BIRDS OF PREY

# Peregrine FALCONS

by Melissa Hill

Consulting Editor: Gail Saunders-Smith, PhD

Consultant: Jessica Ehrgott, Bird and Mammal Trainer, Downtown Aquarium, Denver

CAPSTONE PRESS
a capstone imprint

Pebble Plus is published by Capstone Press,
1710 Roe Crest Drive, North Mankato, Minnesota 56003
www.capstonepub.com

Copyright © 2015 by Capstone Press, a Capstone imprint. All rights reserved.
No part of this publication may be reproduced in whole or in part, or stored in a retrieval system, or transmitted in any form or by any means, electronic, mechanical, photocopying, recording, or otherwise, without written permission of the publisher.

**Library of Congress Cataloging-in-Publication Data**
Hill, Melissa, 1975–
Peregrine falcons / by Melissa Hill.
pages cm.—(Pebble plus. Birds of Prey)
Includes bibliographical references and index.
Summary: "Describes the characteristics, habitat, behavior, life cycle, and threats to peregrine falcons"—Provided by publisher.
Audience: Ages 5 to 8.
Audience: Grades K to 3.
ISBN 978-1-4914-2092-8 (library binding)
ISBN 978-1-4914-2310-3 (pbk.)
ISBN 978-1-4914-2333-2 (ebook pdf)
1. Peregrine falcon—Juvenile literature. I. Title.
QL696.F34H55 2014
598.9′6—dc23 2014032782

**Editorial Credits**
Jeni Wittrock, editor; Peggie Carley and Janet Kusmierski, designers; Svetlana Zhurkin, media researcher; Katy LaVigne, production specialist

**Photo Credits**
Alamy: blickwinkel, 5; Minden Pictures: Konrad Wothe, 7, Martin Dohrn, 15; Newscom: Photoshot/NHPA/Alan Williams, 17, Photoshot/NHPA/Dave Watts, 19; Shutterstock: balounm, back cover (background), Chris Hill, 1, 9, Michael G. McKinne, cover, back cover, Steve Oehlenschlager, 11, StockPhotoAstur, 13, taviphoto, 21

## Note to Parents and Teachers

The Birds of Prey set supports national science standards related to life science. This book describes and illustrates peregrine falcons. The images support early readers in understanding the text. The repetition of words and phrases helps early readers learn new words. This book also introduces early readers to subject-specific vocabulary words, which are defined in the Glossary section. Early readers may need assistance to read some words and to use the Table of Contents, Glossary, Read More, Internet Sites, Critical Thinking Using the Common Core, and Index sections of the book.

Printed in the United States 5553

# Table of Contents

Feathered Predator . . . . . 4
Up Close! . . . . . 8
Living on the Edge . . . . . 14
Falcon Families . . . . . 16
Glossary . . . . . 22
Read More . . . . . 23
Internet Sites . . . . . 23
Critical Thinking Using the Common Core . . . . . 24
Index . . . . . 24

# Feathered Predator

A hunting peregrine falcon flies high. It spots a smaller bird below. The peregrine dives fast and grabs its meal with its feet.

When diving, peregrines are faster than any other animal. They may dive up to 200 miles (322 kilometers) per hour. That is fast!

# Up Close!

Smooth gray feathers cover a peregrine's back. The falcon's underside has spots and stripes. Its head and cheeks are dark.

Strong chests and wings
help peregrines fly fast.
Their pointed wings slice
through the air.

Peregrines have long toes and talons to catch and hold prey. Sharp, curved beaks are perfect for eating meat. Peregrines' main prey is birds.

# Living on the Edge

Peregrine falcons live all over the world. Peregrines are found in deserts, grasslands, and even in cities.

# Falcon Families

Many birds build nests with sticks. Not peregrines! They choose a high, rocky place to lay their eggs.

Peregrine falcons lay two
to four eggs each year.
In a month the eggs hatch.
Peregrine chicks learn to fly
and hunt in two months.

Life isn't easy for a falcon. They can be hurt or killed by great horned owls and people. Wild peregrines can live 10 or more years.

# Glossary

**beak**—the hard front part of the mouth of a bird

**chick**—a young bird

**prey**—an animal that is hunted by another animal for food

**slice**—to move or cut through something smoothly and easily

**talon**—a sharp, curved claw

**underside**—the part of a bird's body that usually faces the ground

# Read More

**Jessell, Tim.** *Falcon.* New York: Random House Books, 2012.

**Lunis, Natalie.** *Peregrine Falcon: Dive, Dive, Dive!* New York: Bearport Pub., 2010.

**Sill, Cathryn P.** *About Raptors.* About Series. Atlanta: Peachtree Publishers, 2010.

# Internet Sites

FactHound offers a safe, fun way to find Internet sites related to this book. All of the sites on FactHound have been researched by our staff.

Here's all you do:

Visit *www.facthound.com*

Type in this code: 9781491420928

# Critical Thinking Using the Common Core

What are the main dangers to peregrine falcons? (Key Ideas and Details)

How might peregrine falcons escape from predators? (Integration of Knowledge and Ideas)

# Index


beaks, 12
cheeks, 8
chests, 10
chicks, 18
colors, 8
diving, 4, 6
eating, 12
eggs, 16, 18, 20
feathers, 8
feet, 4, 12
head, 8
homes, 14, 16
hunting, 4, 18
life span, 20
nests, 16, 18
owls, 20
people, 20
prey, 4, 12
speed, 6, 10
talons, 12
toes, 12
underside, 8
wings, 10



**Word Count: 191**
**Grade: 1**
**Early-Intervention Level: 14**